The Lotus flower is sacred. It's the only flower that seeds and blooms at the same time. This symbolizes the universal law of Cause and Effect. At the moment that we create a cause, an effect exists.

The lotus only blooms in the muddy swamp, which symbolizes the general circumstances of people's lives. You don't need to be in ideal conditions to bloom.

The Ying Yang is a duality. This duality symbolizes life expression. Opposite forces allow for balance. No darkness, no growth. No light, no awareness.

Our existence is either the ego or the true self. That's the duality to be experienced in life.

The Lotus blossom and Yin Yang together express the truth of our existence. We're all one. One force. One life.

Our struggles help us to develop compassion for ourselves and others.

Claim Your Happiness

Practical Poetry for Life, Love and Self

Adil Panton

BALBOA.PRESS
A DIVISION OF HAY HOUSE

Copyright © 2021 Adil Panton.

All rights reserved. No part of this book may be used or reproduced by any means, graphic, electronic, or mechanical, including photocopying, recording, taping or by any information storage retrieval system without the written permission of the author except in the case of brief quotations embodied in critical articles and reviews.

Balboa Press books may be ordered through booksellers or by contacting:

Balboa Press
A Division of Hay House
1663 Liberty Drive
Bloomington, IN 47403
www.balboapress.com
844-682-1282

Because of the dynamic nature of the Internet, any web addresses or links contained in this book may have changed since publication and may no longer be valid. The views expressed in this work are solely those of the author and do not necessarily reflect the views of the publisher, and the publisher hereby disclaims any responsibility for them.

The author of this book does not dispense medical advice or prescribe the use of any technique as a form of treatment for physical, emotional, or medical problems without the advice of a physician, either directly or indirectly. The intent of the author is only to offer information of a general nature to help you in your quest for emotional and spiritual well-being. In the event you use any of the information in this book for yourself, which is your constitutional right, the author and the publisher assume no responsibility for your actions.

Any people depicted in stock imagery provided by Getty Images are models, and such images are being used for illustrative purposes only.
Certain stock imagery © Getty Images.

Print information available on the last page.

ISBN: 978-1-9822-7168-8 (sc)
ISBN: 978-1-9822-7170-1 (hc)
ISBN: 978-1-9822-7169-5 (e)

Library of Congress Control Number: 2021914373

Balboa Press rev. date: 10/11/2021

This book is dedicated to my parents, Maria and Herman Panton.

Mother Maria Panton who taught me not to complain and to honor common sense.

Father Herman Panton for teaching me to be a man of my word and sincerely care for my family and all people.

Acknowledgement

Leslie Panton

Your love, strength and pioneering spirit got us out of the cold
into the land of the golden sun, where we've been
able to develop, strive and succeed as a family.
We love you dearly and I am eternally grateful for you.

Asanti & Cezanne

Your contributions to the development of this
book brought me joy I will always cherish.
You both hold intellect and wisdom beyond your age
that I continue to look forward to experiencing.
Asanti: I adore your generosity, compassion
and great communication skills.
Cezanne: I admire your independent spirit, courage and strength.
I am so proud of you both.

Fatima, Aswad, Raish, Nahlia & Ishara

I enjoy being in your lives for all these years and sharing with you
all that we have passed through together.
You will always be in my heart.

Nazen Zora

Your gift of an elegant journal started the writing process resulting in the messages from my heart found in this book. Your logo design beautifully reflects my life's mission. Thanks for bringing my ideas and thoughts to light and putting them into form.

Esther Wright

Your generosity and belief in my spoken words made the future the present and the book in me a reality.

Cynthia Rast

I truly appreciate you for having the courage of tackling the task of transposing and organizing my written words. Your kindness is immeasurable.

Rita Robinson

Your tenacity in providing clarity with your editing skills was indispensable. It allowed me to breathe easily because you were there to correct my course.

Laura Gatlin

You are an amazing force, an angel who kept
the project moving to the end.
A gift that arrived right on time and kept on giving.
Sincere appreciation and respect for your
invaluable efforts and collaboration.

Sakina Ibrahim

Your gift of a great resource for the book's design
made the completed work beautiful.
Your Light continues to lead to great answers.

Todd Rapparport

Capturing a moment of tremendous joy for my
bio photo is priceless and precious.
Truly a treasure I will enjoy forever. Your consistent,
genuine support is greatly appreciated.

Curtisha Thomas

Because of your book design and layout talents,
Claim Your Happiness has come to fruition.
The style and depth you brought to this book was
beyond my imagination. I am deeply grateful.

Jessie Dean

Like a true brother in faith, I can always count

on you. Your constant friendship,

resourcefulness, capabilities and camaraderie

provide support and answers

just when they're needed. Thanks for being my friend.

And to all my family, clients, students and friends

You are the reason and the inspiration for every word in this book.

Because of you, the wisdom came through me, not from me.

Thank you for providing an endless river of spirited connection.

Contents

Acknowledgement vii

Introduction xxi

LIFE

The Symphony of Life 1

Rhythm of Life 2

True Humanity 3

Reality 4

Stretch 5

Well-Schooled 6

Simple, Not Easy 7

Afraid of Each Other 8

Shine Where You Stand 9

No Problem 10

One True Thought 11

Listening to Life Closely 12

Embrace Infinity 13

Mastership 14

Happy to Be Here 15

Peace 16

Livin' Is Easy 17

Zombie 18

Bloom Where You Stand	19
Equality	20
Mystery Is Mystic	21
Thus I Heard In Silence (meditation)	22
Moving On	23
What You Don't Know	24
Smart, Ain't It?	25
Mission Possible	26
Your Purpose	27
True Freedom	28
Breathe Deeply	29
Free Yourself	30
Skin Deep	31
Beyond	32
To Breathe	33
Answer	34
Pure Land	35
Greatest Good	36
Time	37
Broaden	38
It's All for Us	39
No Ego	40
The Power to Create	41
Karmic DNA	42
Great Heart	43

Focus on Your Breath and Breathe Deeply 44

It's Not Personal 45

*You Are Life Force 46

More 47

Unity 48

Mystic 49

Paint Your Life 50

Impatience Is Not A Flower 51

We Are Timeless 52

Personal Wish 53

Oneness 54

Balance, Not Perfection 55

Still to See 56

Breakthrough 57

Change Now 58

Happiness Before Unhappiness 59

Chasing the Carrot 60

Absolute Happiness 61

Reality 62

Lighten Up 63

Dark Light 64

Patience 65

Ego or Life, that Is the Question 66

Is That Fun? 67

Take Care, This Life May Last Forever 68

Life Is Truth 69

Believe It or Not 70

You Talk Too Much 71

Mind Less 72

Wealth 73

The Challenges of Life 74

Timeless 75

LOVE

Diamond Palace 79

True Love 80

Love Is Strong 81

Self-hate 82

What You Give 83

True Happiness 84

What Is Love? 85

Resolve 86

Moving On 87

First Things First 88

Depth 89

Recovery 90

Power of Peace 91

Eternity 92

Be There 93

Risk It	94
The End	95
Living to be Happy	96
Excellent	97
Next	98
The Star In Your Mirror	99
Love for Hate	100
Necessary Self-Care	101
Supreme Being Within	102
Love Isn't	103
Thrive	104
Self-Love, Loving Life	105
Push and Shove	106
Trust	107
Wholeness	108
Unconditional Love	109
The Challenge	110
Appreciate	111
Self-love	112
Be Whole	113
Loving Life	114
The Heart of Love	115
Twin Breath	116
It's Not Personal	117
Essential Love	118

Powerful Soul 119

Life purpose 120

The Quest of Love 121

Appreciation 122

Desire 123

Universal 124

Center 125

Love 126

Answers 127

My Life 128

Promise 129

Anticipation 130

SELF

The True Self 133

BIG 134

Clarity Is Power 135

Say What? 136

Attachment 137

Mystic 138

Good Vibration 139

No Drama, No Trauma 140

Transformation 141

Existential 142

I'm Great	143
Give It Time	144
Infinity and Beyond	145
Pay Attention	146
It's Just a Story	147
Awesome	148
Let E-Go	149
Greatness	150
To Be Afraid	151
Unbroken Truth	152
Polish Your Presence	153
Fools Waiting to be Wise	154
Finding Your Place	155
Be	156
Embodiment	157
Light	158
Inadequate	159
Action	160
Intentions	161
No Excuses	162
Birthday Wish	163
You	164
Top Crimes	165
Appreciate	166
Best Part of You	167

Self-enslaved	168
No Mind	169
Your Power	170
The Path Least Traveled	171
Who Am I?	172
I Am	173
Moving Up	174
Your Own Private Idaho	175
Ego Is An Evil Master	176
You Are In Control	177
Human Revolution	178
The Gift	179
Fear	180
The Mystic Law	181
Acceptance	182
Solution	183
Response-Able	184
Don't Think, Breathe	185
We Are All Great	186
Shine On	187
Use Your Voice	188
Buying Fear Is Optional	189
Don't Give It Away	190
Think Not	191
Fear Not	192

Master Your Mind	193
Finding You	194
Instead	195
That Was Easy	196
No Regrets	197
Personal Responsibility	198
The Pleasure of Pain	199
State of Origin	200
Master Your Mind	201
No Worries, No Regrets	202
Change	203
Pledge to Self	204
Never Say "I'll Try"	205
No Excuses	206
Know Thy Self	207
Truth in Beauty	208
Entitlement	209
You Are More	210
Be Still	211
To Complain	212
Self-Worth	213
Maximum	214
Clarity	215
The Burden	216
About the Author	217

Introduction

I met Adil Panton as a Qigong teacher. I was frazzled energetically and the idea of taking a Qigong class just popped into my mind. I had never taken one before. I looked it up online and found a class that night at a nearby center. I was there.

I followed his slow yet unfamiliar movements, trying to stay with the rest of the class, most of whom were long-time students. As he moved through his sequence, he was saying things that were hitting me right on the head, things I needed to hear that uncannily were addressing my current situation of dealing with of a derailed adult child that was breaking open my heart, a self-revealing personal relationship that was cracking open my mind and a long-time job that was finally getting under my skin. What he said, surprisingly, was extremely calming.

After the hour class, I felt like I had gotten eight hours of sound sleep, completely renewed, energetic and revived. And good, long, uninterrupted sleep was hard to come by for me at that time. I asked Adil if he said those same things at every class. He said no, he's inspired each time by his students. I have since learned that he lets the wisdom come through him as he tunes into each individual.

The same is true with the poems in this book. They were inspired by his students, clients and colleagues and the wisdom comes through him.

At the end of the class, I also asked him what else he did because teaching Qigong couldn't be the only thing he did. He said he was a full-time massage therapist. I immediately said I needed a massage, which I desperately did for the reasons mentioned above.

When I got my first massage from him, he asked me what was going on with my daughter. I hadn't yet talked about my daughter. I asked him how he knew. He said I had a knot the size of an egg on the left side of my neck, usually connected to female children. Right on. I said I was about to divorce her as I had done the rest of my family due to exasperation and what I considered very bad behavior.

He said I couldn't do that. Why? Because your family picks you and you pick your family to work out certain circumstances that may be generations, even centuries old. If you don't clear it in this lifetime, you're going to start all over with it in the next. Oh, man. I didn't want to go through any of it again. I asked him what he based that philosophy on and he told me about Nichiren Buddhism, a Buddhist practice from the 13th Century that chants Nam Myo Renge Kyo to clear ages-old karma in this lifetime, uplift your life condition and receive the wisdom you need to live the life you want to live here and now. I was intrigued. I went to my first intro meeting the next week and received my Gohonzon, a mandala or scroll used to focus our chanting, two weeks later. The

Gohonzon is scripted with the energy of the Mystic Law or the universal law of cause and effect. Very simply stated, you make good causes, you get good results. You make bad causes, bad results. When your life condition is positive and solid, you usually make good decisions.

The beautiful thing I like about chanting is that you can leave your worries, fears, heartbreaks and concerns with the Gohonzon and let the universe receive your vibration and return the situations and the wisdom to act in those situations to your and others' greatest benefit.

I now understand that Adil's Buddhist practice gives him the clarity of mind and the purity of heart and spirit to be able to receive the wisdom his students and clients need to hear. That's a true, unpretentious healer, being open to the universal truth that surrounds all of us and is available to everyone as their vibration and spirit rises to meet it.

Please enjoy the wisdom found in these pages. I'm sure there's some that will hit you over the head, too.

Rita Robinson
Writer, editor, environmentalist

ADIL PANTON

POEMS ON

Life

The Symphony of Life

Mastering your mind is simply making up your mind to succeed.

Life wants you to win.

The challenge is aligning yourself with this awareness.

Life is one big symphony. We all have our part to play.

Your part to play is you.

Play it well.

The challenge is having the courage to play our part.

There is only one conductor—Life itself.

Follow the cues by tuning in.

We hear the conductor and are in rhythm with life.

Creating balance and harmony in the symphony of life.

Everyone plays their part well.

By becoming truly happy, no one can lose in the symphony of life.

Rhythm of Life

Death, the End and new Beginning.
In the Circle of Life,
words are sound notes when spoken correctly as the ability to compassionately create peace and happiness.
You are more than your thoughts.
Each moment of life is precious.
Live them with deep appreciation.
Accept the good and bad, fully experiencing life as it presents itself.

True Humanity

How can we be a better human?
Identify with only one race: the human race.
For all shades of color, the simple origin is humanity.
To be a racist is to be ignorant of the human being.

Reality

Our mind exists to support our reality,

not dictate our reality.

We create all of our experiences.

Choose what you want to create wisely.

Time is artificial reality.

True reality is eternity.

Celebrate your life today.

Train right.

Eat right.

Live right.

The true beauty of life already exists inside of you.

Celebrate you and bring it forth.

Stretch

Life is a stretch.

Be prepared to grow.

Well-Schooled

Life is the classroom.

Experience is the teacher.

Adversity is a test.

To achieve victory, focus on the resolution, not the problem.

We have many thoughts in a single moment.

However, it's our single action that determines

the outcome of our thoughts.

Thoughts become reality

when we act upon them.

Simple, Not Easy

The solution is usually simple.

The application is hard.

Afraid of Each Other

Why are human beings so fearful and afraid of each other?

Simply, we don't recognize our oneness.

WE ARE ALL Human Beings.

In each other, the gifts of life are the experiences we share.

Shine Where You Stand

Be the sun, not the lamp.

A perfect life is one full of obstacles and victories.

Be still while moving.

No Problem

Problems exist for us to resolve,
not to hang out with or live with.

One True Thought

My one true thought: I am Buddha.

Any other thought is wasted.

Buddha encompasses everything.

Buddha is Life.

Listening to Life Closely

ESP is simply

paying acute attention to the

workings and expressions of life.

The body is an illusionary boundary.

There is no boundary to the true self.

It goes beyond what's seen.

Explore and recognize through the senses.

There is no limitation to what you can see, feel, touch, and hear.

Embrace Infinity

Infinity takes you
wherever you want to go.
Matter is a particular vibration.
That's all.
Come swim in the Universe of
beauty and peace everywhere.
Take the brakes off your life
and live your dreams.

Mastership

Master your impermanent existence,

while knowing you will live forever

as an infinite spirit.

This life is a dream

in which the ultimate truth is compassion.

The ideal life

and desire for world peace

through individual happiness are One...

once we overcome the fear of existence.

Happy to Be Here

Are you breathing?

It's a beautiful day.

Peace

Humanity above issues.

Livin' Is Easy

If you solidify your existence by syncing with life's vibration, you can have it all.

Zombie

Today people are walking dead,

not seeing clearly.

People like to swim in the shallows while wanting the treasures of the deep.

Bloom Where You Stand

Massage opens you up like a flower, allowing you to bloom.

Life is a journey,

giving us the lessons we are able to learn,

and not attaching to what's temporary.

Equality

One Mind as Mentor,

conquering doubt and fears.

Why must other human beings suffer for a few?

At the end we are all simply human beings

existing on this planet together.

Let's share it equally.

For world peace.

Mystery Is Mystic

Each life,
your life,
is a mystery to be experienced.

Thus I Heard In Silence (meditation)

The Buddha heard the Mystic Law,
bringing the sound forward and realizing.
Opening the door for all to understand,
the great "I am" that unlocks life's mysteries.

Moving On

We are not living to acquire,
but to expire in the best manner.

What You Don't Know

You know not what you don't know.

An accident is simply a lack of awareness.

Instead of swimming aimlessly and erratically in your mind,

swim in the vast ocean of life.

Body, mind and spirit are interdependent, functioning as One.

Smart, Ain't It?

Don't be satisfied with being smart.

Seek to be wise with experience.

Then you cannot be misled.

Wisdom is the ultimate truth in the universe.

Align your heart and mind with the universe.

You will know wisdom and become a victor,

not a victim in life.

Mission Possible

It's impossible to be happy without appreciating your own life.

Your Purpose

Manifest greatness by leading people to happiness.

True freedom

That which you choose to avoid

you must overcome

in order to be truly free.

Breathe Deeply

All problems require breath to be solved.

Relax.

Breathe deeply and open.

free Yourself

With understanding,

there is freedom from the imprisonment of circumstances.

There is perfection in the moment.

How else could the moment exist?

This life is precious and short.

Pursue understanding it, instead of wasting it.

Skin Deep

It's not the color of the skin that makes the human being.
It's the depth of the awareness of the mystery of life.

Beyond

You are more than a human being.

You are a universal being. That's eternity.

To Breathe

Life is all about the breath,

the middle way between

existence and nonexistence.

That which we take for granted

assures us of another moment of existence.

Breathe deeply

and experience the eternity of life.

Answer

History repeats itself
because we are not answering the call
that provides an answer.
All are called, very few answer.

Pure Land

Purify in thought

simplify in action

live forever.

Greatest Good

Accentuate the positive,

recognize the negative.

All exist for our greatest good.

Time

Time is not what determines the outcome.

It's our input that decides.

Tomorrow is not promised.

It's a possibility of true appreciation

for the present moment.

Broaden

The broader your life

the greater your stance

the more balance you have.

It's All for Us

In life, accentuate the positive

and recognize the negative

as a lesson to be learned

and an energy to transform.

No Ego

Suffering is attachment

to less than what is—the eternity of life.

To detach doesn't mean to isolate or separate.

It means to detach from ego and return to the balance of the eternity of life.

The Power to Create

The greatest manifestation of true power is creation.

Karmic DNA

Our DNA is our karmic code.

We are all great spirits on an adventure to reconnect with true self.

The purity of your being is to manifest the ultimate power:

You and the universe are one.

The eternity of life is you.

That cannot be destroyed.

We simply transform.

To believe in one's self is to embrace the ultimate truth of life.

Life is powerful, magnificent, dynamic

and goes beyond this finite reality.

Be careful what you tell yourself about yourself.

Either a truth or a lie affects your outcome.

Great Heart

True freedom—knowledge plus wisdom,

leads to the courage to walk through the doors

of enslavement in body, mind and spirit.

Freedom, desire and intention fueled by prayer provide strength.

Prayer is the consistent focus.

Strong prayer is single-minded focus with passion.

Truly listen to your heart and let your mind follow.

For the great heart knows all the great answers to the mysteries of life.

We come into life with the tendency of not knowing

then live our life convincing ourselves of what we already know.

Focus on Your Breath and Breathe Deeply

Breath is life itself, in its purest form.

All breathe and live, experiencing the oneness of life.

The commonality of all things is breathing.

Allow your breath to become your mind.

Focus on breath and watch your life expand.

Experience being in rhythm with life itself.

It's Not Personal

Accept the experience.

*You Are Life force

How do you start your day?

Start the day with the fact that you are life—powerful and dynamic.

Stop looking in the rearview mirror of your life when you are wanting to move forward.

Your hardship is training you for your leadership.

Every day that you sit in the meditation of self-awareness,

you are in training to increase your ability to command universal life force.

More

Be present to the gift of life,

for every moment is an opportunity for more.

To be of true service to humanity,

be able to relate to humanity.

In order to relate to humanity,

you must experience pain.

Humanity comes from traveling through a sea of suffering.

Unity

Get out of your head and step boldly into your life.

One mind.

One heart.

One destiny.

Unity.

Mystic

Transform your ignorance into light.

Your arrogance into humility. Uniting with your human soul.

For we are all simply one.

Star lights of the infinite universe rediscovering self.

Single-mindedly focus on the truth that exists deep inside you.

We are born with truth buried in the breast of our hearts.

When discovered, it will free us from the flames of pain.

Let today count for greatness in your life.

Creating tomorrow is taking care of today.

To be seen and heard will strengthen your life force.

Paint Your Life

Time is an empty canvas we paint on every day.

What will you paint today?

I am Life.

Who I am and what I am.

Nothing more, nothing less.

Simply Life for all of eternity.

If you separate part of you from the whole,

an empty hole is what remains.

Impatience Is Not A Flower

A flower does not rush to bloom.

If you persist in being impatient,

the probability exists that you will become a patient.

The goal in life isn't perfection.

It's balance.

Perfection creates stress.

Balance creates peace and harmony.

We Are Timeless

In the true aspect of life, your spirit is timeless.
Every day we live
is an opportunity to understand the purpose
and meaning of life.

Personal Wish

I am Buddha.

Let me save all people from suffering.

Heal myself,

heal my family,

now and for all eternity.

Oneness

Life is existence and nonexistence.

Both unique aspects of the oneness.

To cling to existence

as if there is no other reality is to be deluded.

You must consider both aspects interchangeably

to gain a humble understanding of life.

Balance, Not Perfection

Perfection is a delusion
when life's meaning and intent is balance.

Still to See

Be still and make a wonderful decision for your life.

There, you will find wisdom within your reach.

The word "presence" is essence moving forward.

Breakthrough

There is no escape in life.
You have to breakthrough.
There is no escaping reality.
Simply transform it with courage.

Change Now

The state of life you die in is how you are reborn.

Wisdom of the ages states that in life you reap what you sow.

Happiness Before Unhappiness

Happiness is a prerequisite for unhappiness.

Why chase what you already possess?

Simply determine to be happy... no matter what.

Chasing the Carrot

Perfection is the unattainable carrot.

Life is balance.

Not chasing the carrot.

There is no great life

without obstacles.

Obstacles lift us to have a winning life.

Absolute Happiness

F - Family of humanity

U - Unity of true purpose

N - Never-give-up spirit

= true happiness.

True happiness isn't possible without a problem to solve.

If you are not struggling,

the opportunity to discover more of your great self is lost.

Simply go beyond your mind

and step into the center of your life.

Keep smiling, the sun is still shining.

In life today, ignorance is the norm and arrogance is the elite.

Let your actions do the talking.

What's the greatest thing that exists under the sun?

Life. My life. Your life. All life.

Reality

Death walks with me just as life does.

Both are inseparable,

as fish and water.

This is Buddhahood.

The Lotus Sutra goes beyond the mundane

into the supremacy of life.

Then back to the mundane

for its manifestation of the joy of life.

Lighten Up

Let your heart be your light

so you can be present.

Put yourself at ease,

seek balance and experience joy.

True life: the sun always rises.

False life: snowflakes that simply evaporate.

Become truth.

Dark Light

Don't let the light in your life be darkness.

Illuminate your life with brightness.

Resolve to be the sun.

Patience

Time is patience.

Patience is taking time without haste.

Ego or Life, that Is the Question

There is nothing wrong with ego
other than it puts itself above life.
Put your ego into check by remaining centered in life.

Is That fun?

People are committed to having fun

at any price.

Yet their method ends up causing pain to themselves and others.

Sometimes this pain is irreparable.

When did having fun

become more valuable than life?

Take Care, This Life May Last Forever

This life is a short journey on the long road of eternity.

Be mindful of your destination and walk vigilantly.

Recognizing that the steps you take today create the path of your

future into eternity.

Life Is Truth

Recognize everything

and identify only with life.

For life is the ultimate truth and reality.

Believe It or Not

In life, the most unfavorable experiences
tend to us more than the good experiences.
This is where the most precious jewels in life are found.

You Talk Too Much

Why is it that those who talk a lot
tend to know less than they think they do?
They would be better off being quiet
and simply listening.

Mind Less

If you rely on your mind to do your best,

you will fall short.

Doing your best comes from the depths.

Because life knows more about your capability

than the mind.

Doing your best is not for your mind to decide.

It's that which only you can decide.

Ultimately your life is bigger than your mind.

Step into the true reality of your existence.

Rely on your life and not only the mind.

Life is the ultimate truth.

Simply embrace it with all its challenges

to make you have a great human experience.

Wealth

In order to live a rich, full life, simply reclaim your true state
—happiness.

The Challenges of Life

Become the master of your mind.

Be the observer of your thoughts and only entertain those that are fruitful to your true soulful intention.

Life gives us challenges for us to discover more of ourselves.

There is a lot more emptiness than thought. Emptiness holds the space for thought.

Embrace positive possibility and deflect negative opportunities.

You're not meant to do what's easy.

You're meant to challenge yourself.

Be in the flow of life and doors will open.

Know the body.

Know the universe.

We are motivated to do what's challenging and not what's easy.

Timeless

There is no age to the spirit—only the body.

ADIL PANTON

POEMS ON

Love

Diamond Palace

Build a castle within first.
Then cover it with illumination.
A diamond palace.
Love yourself first before seeking love elsewhere.
Stop wondering about what you already possess.
Love is a sincere, deep appreciation of self.
A true seeker of love must commit to looking inside first.
Start love there.
Open the door to the palace within.
First things first.

True Love

The love you seek

give to yourself first.

Don't use the void in you as an excuse to seek love outside of yourself.

It will fail.

Be still and let love be you.

If true love is not on the inside,

what you experience on the outside is an illusion.

Is it time to awaken?

If you're doing your best in the moment,

then you can only be fruitful. Doing your best is love.

Love Is Strong

Like a tree,

the deeper the root,

the greater the ability to bear the sweet fruit of love.

Self-hate

Condemnation of self only increases pain.

Learn to resonate with love of self

in order to break the cycle of pain.

Love of self must become a practice.

Practice makes it possible

for thoughts, words, and action

to be congruent with the natural state of love.

Life will work for you.

Life becomes fulfilling when you pay close attention.

What You Give

The Giver is always giving.

Who takes care of the Giver?

Of course, the Giver.

What you give to others also give to yourself.

This is the true heart of giving.

True Happiness

Ultimately, we all want to be happy.

Keep it simple.

Awaken to the infinite compassion in you by loving yourself.

To love yourself is to appreciate the mystic law of life energy,

life's vibration.

They are one and the same—

loving yourself puts you in sync with life's vibration.

It allows you to experience the wonders of life in every moment,

for life's wonders to come to you in every moment.

In stillness there is power.

In balance there is strength.

In movement there is flexibility.

I am here to discover what I already possess within me.

Love once again.

What Is Love?

True love waits.

It doesn't become restless and go astray.

Love yourself more.

First, give yourself the love you are wanting to give away.

Then you will have more to genuinely give to others.

Resolve

Prayer is simply a resolve.

The strength of your resolve determines the outcome.

Utilize your mind to manifest what your heart intends.

You cannot find

what you are not looking for.

Moving On

Tomorrow is made by today.

Know the answer before you die.

Still your mind

so you can perceive what's in your heart.

First Things First

Everyone is seeking love and understanding.

Why not love and understand yourself first?

Then be about the business of sharing.

Depth

No matter how deep the mind is,

it's still shallow.

When you consider the depth of the ocean—the heart.

Be silent and go deep.

Recovery

Love life more than your vices.

Power of Peace

Courage, compassion, wisdom, harmony.

Power runs through our veins

when love is in our hearts.

A uniting force

for good overcoming all obstacles in our personal life.

Standing up for justice,

bringing hope to the people in our native land

and sheltering them from harm.

We are united in peace, love, justice, and happiness.

Conquering all our fears.

We live and breathe harmony.

Eternity

The Power to Be

moves through me and with me.

I love forever more for all eternity

Be There

Wherever you run, there you are.

If you want peace,

resolve to be courageous and solve your problems.

What is true about you is unfamiliar.

Love.

Be that.

Risk It

Fear assists love.

Because to love is to be vulnerable. Which sometimes feels like fear.

Isn't it a risk worth taking?

The End

In the end, love and be love.

Let life embrace you

with its true wonder—Love.

Living to be Happy

No time to wait.

The time is now.

Advance for world peace.

Powerfully and happily.

Peace resides in your heart, in your actions.

Actions to change the world from pain and destruction.

All live and be free.

Free from attachment.

Excellent

Guided by a sincere heart,
we achieve excellence in ourselves.

Next

I am not tired for

I am alive.

When I grow tired, I will die and recharge for my next life.

What's the purpose of my existence?

Is it to suffer and not be fully aware?

No.

It's to manifest greatness in the physical form.

Unite the dimension of one's existence—body, mind, and spirit.

Coming together and expressing the divine state of true love.

The Star In Your Mirror

If you can feed your weakness the same disbelieve of self,

how can you believe in self?

Your delusions will only manifest less-than-fulfilling conclusions.

You are the ultimate truth in life.

Commit to being the truth and your days will remain bright.

You are a star among stars.

Be the star you already are.

Shine brilliantly.

Your greatest good is what you tell yourself about yourself.

It's your internal motivator for all of your actions.

It is how you appear to others.

Love for Hate

Instead of adding to your problem,

subtract from your problem and find a solution.

What's absent from hate is love.

Pour love into hate

and it purifies and brings forth a true state of being—love.

Love is the answer to human suffering.

Necessary Self-Care

There's no excuse for not taking care of yourself.
At some point you will simply blow a fuse.
Self-care every day for a better way.

Supreme Being Within

There is so much more we can do and manifest.

Simply dig deeper inside yourself.

Find your treasure within.

You are truly a love supreme.

All challenges are opportunities for self-discovery and growth.

Love Isnt

Love is not the violation of one's spirit, verbal or physical.

Love is not physical or emotional abuse,

no excuse.

Thrive

Change your attitude.

Change your destiny.

Aspire to live and not just survive.

Free yourself from the slavery of your mind

by developing your intuition,

what your heart is saying.

Listen to the true voice that's deeper and quieter within.

The voice that truly wants you to win,

be safe and love sincerely.

Self-Love, Loving Life

When you fall in love with yourself
everything else is possible.
A winning life is seeking balance while struggling.

Push and Shove

Whenever you push

the natural response is resistance.

However, when you are open,

there is allowance.

Those who love themselves

treat the world differently, kindly.

Trust

Trust life,
it will always provide what you need.
Simply learn to pay attention.
The love you seek
first give to yourself.
Then the love you have
will be fulfilling.

Wholeness

All is matter and matter is the whole.

All that matters is the heart,

the heart that believes in one self.

Without the heart, there is a hole.

Unconditional Love

True expression of unconditional love—the air we breathe.
It keeps on giving and asks nothing in return.
Race, gender, ethnicity, and nationality
are inconsequential factors.
The primary factor is the human being.

The Challenge

Challenge is an opportunity for victory.
There is more to you on the inside than the outside.
So why are you so focused on the outside?
You can only change the past by being present.
Guilt is an illusion that simply weighs you down.
Death is the physical absence of life that
doesn't extinguish the essence of life.
For just like the air we breathe,
life is forever.
If you can't forgive, you can't heal.
Love yourself more than your ego and simply forgive.

Appreciate

Appreciate the past for the lessons you've learned.

Appreciate the present for what you have accomplished.

Appreciate the future for the beauty it will bring.

Let your heart be full of appreciation so that your mind remains clear.

Self-love

When you love yourself,

you create beauty by your very presence.

If you continue to let ego beat you throughout your life,

there is no way to cultivate a winning life.

Life is merciful, it will work with you if you allow it.

Life isn't hard,

if you are willing.

One's life is bigger than the mind.

Depend on life, not the mind.

The miracle of life is body, mind and spirit in complete alliance.

If you truly love yourself

then practice becoming the master of the mind.

An unmastered mind can be easily distracted and influenced.

The pen is mightier than the sword

because of its ability to cultivate a loving heart.

In every moment there is an opportunity to engage with life forever.

Be Whole

Forgiveness is creating wholeness in you

which has been broken.

If you breathe deeply enough,

you will find the answer.

Loving Life

The greatest hardship allows us to manifest the greatest strength.

Step into your loving heart and out of your powerful head.

Wisdom can only flow from having faith.

Suffering is attachment. Love is the freedom.

Faith is the unseen that you believe in, then make into reality.

Get out of your head and into the flow of life.

There is no strength without resistance.

I am in love with life itself. With all its ups and downs.

True love goes beyond this life. On into eternity.

The Heart of Love

The law is true love.
It's solid, never broken, and constantly nurturing—
resonating from the heart—
creating joy, peace, and happiness.

Twin Breath

Every breath I take
the next one is for you.
I want to come home to your loving arms.
Look into your loving smile and face.
Experience joy beyond time and space.

It's Not Personal

When you forgive yourself
for reacting to a person or situation in a way that causes you pain,
you're no longer affected by past painful situations
or anything that might be similar
to it now or yet to come.
If you're still carrying around a wound
and a similar situation occurs and you're triggered,
you have not forgiven yourself.
If you forgive and a similar situation occurs
that could be painful and you're no longer affected by it,
the old wound has been healed.
The trick is not to take it personally.
And then see if there's something to be learned.
Don't carry the pain around as if the old,
painful situation is occurring today.
The fact that you're still standing means you're capable to do
more than you've experienced from past limiting situations.

Essential Love

Life is love and love is me. This is Buddha mastership.

Powerful Soul

To know me
Is to love me.
For my true concern is you.
Your ultimate happiness is always on my mind.
Therefore I will do anything for you;
bring you comfort and try to ease the pain.
Help you to see that no matter what you are going through, that under it all life's heartbeat remains the same.
Beautiful, strong, and majestic.
So rise and be the Queen that you truly are.
Let the true self rise to the occasion and put all illusion aside.
Life is beautiful and so are you.
No matter what you are going through.
Breathe and release yourself in knowing that everything in your life is a blessing for you to change and grow into the person that you truly want to be.
Happy, capable, beautiful, sincere, and free of your Illusions.
For you, realize that life is beautiful no matter what it is that you are going through.
In your heart, this must be your eternal song.
Life is beautiful, no matter what it is that I have to go through.
Life is beautiful and so am I.
I smile and wipe the tears from my eyes
because I am truly in love with all of my life.

Life purpose

My life purpose is to bring joy, happiness, show love, and share love.

Help everyone to understand the true meaning of love.

A feeling that no matter what, everything is going to be alright.

My heart is like the Universe

so vast and wide,

through which the ocean of love flows.

My mission is to reassure you that everything is fine.

With deep faith In the Mystic Law,

we can overcome any obstacle.

Walk with me and come to understand the way of the

Mystic Law that exists inside of you eternally.

Shout, scream Nam Myoho Renge Kyo - the true essence of us all.

The Quest of Love

Love, the need of each and every.
The common bond between all human beings, that
infamous spoken word "love."
In each and every soul is the need for love. Look into the
eyes the window of the soul and deep down you will find love.
Hoping and wanting to be free.
It does not matter who you are, or where you have been.

For the sake of love, be free...

Appreciation

No human being should be discouraged by another human being.

We should all strive to uplift each other's spirit.

For so precious is each and everyone's life.

Filled with so much energy and ability.

Let's build one another and bring joy to each other's life.

With sincere appreciation,

I share my life with you.

Desire

Free from the restrictions in my MIND.
Living life fully.
Enjoying every moment,
be it pain, joy, or sorrow.
Extending myself to you.
Exploring my sensitivity.
Understanding what it really means to be a Man:
capable, sincere, and devoted in the way of TRUTH.
Manifesting all that is beautiful within.
Disregarding all that is negative.
Caring so patiently.
Wanting the union of body, mind, and soul.
This I Desire.

Universal

The Sun my Father.

The Moon my Mother.

The Stars my Brothers and Sisters.

And all other planetary entities are within me.

Throughout eternity I have always existed.

That ray of Hope.

Shining throughout the Universe,

shedding light on the essence of all beings.

That has always been just as me.

Center

For the light in me shines when I breathe.

In the stillness of the night, true self is expressed when I let the heart speak.

Confused I am not when I let the heart speak.

All is peaceful and calm at the Center of my Life.

Love

Is a feeling that one must maintain,

in order to express true humanity.

For what is at the root of the world's suffering?

None other than true love lost in the annals of human history.

It is the true desire of all human beings to be loved.

For what is it that makes one truly happy?

The ability to love and be loved.

In our hearts, we all seek love.

It is the lantern in the dark,

the companion when lonely,

and the answer when in doubt.

LOVE.

The true generator and Spirit of all LIVES.

Answers

Are all within.
The ability to dig deep enough
takes courage and patience.

My Life

This life

Just!

What is life?

A cumulation of endless moments,

in which there is joy and sorrow.

Promise

To seek the answer
to this love in my heart for you.

Anticipation

Concern for tomorrow

is the faith to believe and to carry on.

Seeking the truth in everything.

How does one open their eyes?

And see the reality—all is real as far as one can see.

ADIL PANTON

POEMS ON

Self

The True Self

The true self is never dubious.
It's direct.
In stillness it whispers,
never competing with the inferior, negative mind.
Always calm and serene, it speaks the truth,
direct and appropriate, with self-awareness.
Straight from the heart.
Simply listen.
You already know the truth.
You are the truth.

BIG

Intuitively, we know that our lives are big.

Yet we keep ourselves small

because of the lack of courage

and the influence of others,

whose hearts have been broken.

They speak to us from the position of a broken heart.

Courage is the key for a winning life.

The lion's roar expresses courage.

Courage to breakthrough our self-imposed limitations.

Faith and courage are the same thing.

What you tell yourself about yourself is who you are.

Having faith in yourself will give you courage to trust life.

Manifest right thought, right speech, right action—

Be aware of what you are affirming.

Be the master of your mind.

To master your mind means to purify your mind.

A purified mind easily perceives the Buddha.

If you can see the Buddha,

then you can see yourself.

Clarity Is Power

The ability to see clearly allows you to achieve.
Clarity gives you the power to become
a genuine and sincere human being.

Say What?

Your life's challenges are demanding you to manifest your greatness.

If you can enjoy what you have,

you actually make room to have even more.

Attachment

Attachment erodes happiness.

It only serves the ego.

Detach your ego from the outcome, not your love.

Be happy now.

Come alive for all humanity to see so they can believe.

No more self-destruction.

Construct a happy, vibrant self.

Do it now.

Mystic

The Mystic Law

Is life itself.

With all the wonders of existence,

I commit to paper the magic that flows out of me.

My gift to the world of each and every one of us,

Is to intrinsically enlighten beings.

Good Vibration

First there is sound
that stimulates thought,
which brings forth frequency that vibrates.
The frequency of vibration gives birth to our
experiences that become reality.
We create our reality.

No Drama, No Trauma

If you don't want trauma, don't pick up drama.

Gentle spirit,

gentle way,

calm and relaxed.

Proceed with confidence,

walking through the storms of life,

head held high.

Steadily navigating all adversity.

Refusing to lie down until done.

Truth must prevail.

Let it ring in your gentle, confident spirit

loud and clear.

Transformation

When I am Buddha,
all is possible.
I can transform my
reality as I am now,
endowed with infinite
wisdom and compassion
to change my world,
changes the world.
This is human revolution.

Existential

Happiness cannot be
based on what you don't have,
only on what you innately do have.
Help solve the world's problems by taking better care of yourself.
Because each person is a part of the whole body of humankind.

I'm Great

Good isn't good enough

to relieve you of your suffering.

You are great.

Not egotistically,

but as a beautiful, wonderful, loving, compassionate being.

This is our true nature.

Give It Time

At times, those who hurt you the most

are giving you the greatest treasures,

yet it's hard to believe.

Truth is beyond time.

Ultimately, all that matters is truth.

Give it time.

Infinity and Beyond

You are beyond your mind

into infinity,

eternity,

simply use your experiences to find yourself.

Pay Attention

Our experiences are the fruits of our thoughts.

Think big,

take action,

and abundance is yours.

The unknown

is not unknown

to those who act with strength and inner knowingness

and, thus, know courage.

It's Just a Story

Believe in your possibility

and not your history.

Your history doesn't determine your present or future.

It doesn't determine your expectation or outcome.

From this point forward simply decide your possibility.

Awesome

All that there is
is in me.

Let E-Go

Attachment is the mother of suffering.
Detachment means to detach from ego,
Detach from any investment in the return.
It simply means to *let ego go*.

Greatness

Any thought other than "I am great" is a lie we live and tell ourselves.

There is more than enough space on Earth

and in life

for all greatness to coexist peacefully, happily, joyfully.

Consider all the planets just in our universe.

Can you manifest the greatness inside of you?

What's stopping you?

The inferior thoughts you listen to.

Listen only to one true thought:

"I am great no matter what I am going through."

Maintain a high life condition.

To Be Afraid

Thoughts in motion produce emotions.

Being afraid gets you no closer to where you want to be.

Yet we cling to fear as if it's the purpose of our lives.

Nothing can be accomplished

in life without courage.

And courage is simply the absence of fear.

Unbroken Truth

Lost in the myriads of my mind.

Digging deeper to discover all that I am

and all that simply is...

unbroken truth.

Unhappiness comes from depending on things outside of yourself for

your self-worth.

When you dig deep, you'll find answers.

Believe in yourself and provide the answer that creates value.

When a thought comes up,

ask yourself,

"Does this create value?"

Polish Your Presence

There is no enlightenment without problems.

Problems are the catalyst for enlightenment.

Ask yourself:

"Did you polish your presence enough today?"

Are you ready to present the best of you to the world today despite your problems?

Fools Waiting to be Wise

To seek happiness outside of yourself is a guarantee to be disappointed.

At times, we are fools waiting to be wise.

Yet, the deepest pain can make us wise.

Experience equals credibility.

It also beats opinion.

Pain gives us the experience.

Experience gives us the opportunity to see wisdom.

Finding Your Place

Be one with everything

to find one's place.

Stand in the center

and allow everything else

to embrace you.

If you rely on or put your faith in partial truth,

you will be blinded to recognize or know the whole truth

when it is presented.

Be

Transform imagination into reality

by simply believing

there is nowhere to go and nothing to dread.

Just be.

That which is unknown is the real you.

Embodiment

Your physical manifestation is the sum of your whole being.

Not the beginning of your being.

What else is there to do in life but manifest your greatness?

How you speak to yourself is what you experience.

How you speak about others

is what you experience.

Truth is not an easy thing to uphold and share,

especially if you've been living a lie most of your life.

Light

When there is sun,
still be the light.
When there are clouds,
still be the light.

Inadequate

We have the ultimate.
And still, we think we need more.
If you really knew yourself,
would you still be afraid?

Action

We experience thoughts as reality

when we take action to manifest them.

When it occurs to you is the best time to act.

Intentions

By paying attention to intention
you can dramatically change your reality.
What is your intention?

No Excuses

Be courageous and make your mark.
The world awaits your timely presence.

Birthday Wish

To get rid of arrogance and quickly attain Buddhahood,
the way to truth, justice and absolute happiness for oneself
and others is gratitude.
I smile and appreciate all the great lives in my life.

You

When you become the solution, there are no problems that cannot be solved.

Top Crimes

I declare that ignorance and arrogance are the greatest crimes.
Both rob you of your true self.

Appreciate

Because I appreciate life,

I deserve more of this wonderful gift.

Be kind and loving to self.

For self is all you've really got.

Your one and only.

The one true absolute.

Best Part of You

All is not lost,

all just needs to be found.

Self-enslaved

Modern slavery is your own self-imposed limitations,

thoughts and ideas

that paralyze you from moving your life forward.

No Mind

To be free, get your mind out of your way.

Your Power

To call into existence

one's self

is the demonstration of true power.

Now that you are here,

challenge yourself to maintain awareness of your eternal being.

What is the purpose and mission for my being?

This is the question to be answered for a fulfilled life.

The path to a rich experience is to listen deeply within.

Then you will know the purpose and mission of your life.

The Path Least Traveled

A healthy mind and body
provides solutions from the cradle to the grave.
The gift of learning allows you to grow
Time is not what determines your outcome
It is your actions that do.

Who Am I?

Who is that I am?
Fighting my own arrogance,
purifying my life to be truly free.

I Am

The power to be,

to exist in sync with life.

I am that.

Justice will be done.

Moving Up

Youth stand on the shoulders of their parents,

no matter how low it might be,

to achieve more and not less.

Your greatest challenge

is to win over yourself and not the system.

If you can win over yourself, you can deal with the system.

Your Own Private Idaho

What you believe about yourself

is your reality.

If you don't like your reality,

simply strengthen your belief in yourself.

Ego Is An Evil Master

When you are struggling,
the ego is whipping you into shape for suffering.

You Are In Control

Anxiety is fear
running wild in your head.
Stop the madness.

Human Revolution

All other revolutions
other than human revolution
is simply a passing season.
Human revolution is forever.
Don't be afraid to step deep into your truth.
Think kindly of yourself
and stop taxing and aging yourself with negativity.
There is truth in your reality.
However, the ultimate truth is beyond your reality.
You can't go back and fix your past,
there is nothing to fix.
Darkness serves a purpose
so that you can manifest the light.
Life is constantly moving forward.
Stop looking in the rearview mirror of your past to be present.
Be the light.

The Gift

Winners don't beg, complain, blame or give up.

Time is an empty canvas for you to express passion and beauty.

What's your gift?

It's never too late to heal,

for one day of life is worth the effort.

For some people, the most joy your parents experienced

was the gift of making you.

Oh, what a wonderful gift you are.

Fear

Fear is a lack of understanding and awareness of self.

Fear is ultimately a misunderstanding of true self.

Embrace the fear and challenge it.

And there you'll find your strength.

The Mystic Law

The world turns

because of the universal mystic law of life force energy.

Rely on no one,

for the supreme power that resides

is already in you.

Acceptance

Smile and accept life.

Simply breathe and be full of life.

Consider your greatness.

Step into your awareness.

Near and far beyond.

It's time for every person to look into their soul

and create value for the whole.

Love your life more and let go of your impairments today.

The truth already exists inside you.

The power to be great is there for you to manifest.

Whatever problem you may have,

the opportunity exists for you to discover more of your great self.

Solution

Every problem has with it a solution.
The challenge is finding the solution
That already exists within.

Response-Able

It's easier to blame the world and others than take responsibility for
your world.
We are eternal vessels of truth and justice,
here to instill the dignity of human life.
Master your being of everlasting peace and harmony.

Don't Think.

Breathe

Allow your breath to think,
especially when the thinking is not clear.

We Are All Great

There is equal opportunity in the human chain for greatness.

Just like Muhammad Ali.

Simply claim it and work at it.

Shine On

Don't allow your mind to turn to a dark place.

Like flowers,

keep it turned towards the sun.

Use Your Voice

The ultimate weapon of human beings is the voice.

The voice that calls out for truth, justice, love, and happiness.

Why let a few ruin the purpose and dignity of life?

Let your voice be heard.

Buying Fear Is Optional

Those that manufacture weapons of destruction sell fear.

That's the only way they can get you to buy their weapons.

Buying fear is optional.

Arm yourself with the positive forces in life.

Believe in the creative forces.

Walk in the light of love, truth, joy, and happiness.

Don't Give It Away

No one has power over you

other than the power you give them.

We can live our lives being self-conscious or self-aware.

Think Not

People take pride in thinking

and less time on being.

But instead of searching for what is not lost,

be who you truly are.

And shine brightly.

Fear Not

That which human beings fear the most

is the true self because it is mainly unknown.

Just because you want to forget your problems,

does it mean that they are forgotten?

Use your courage to breakthrough.

How else will you discover your true self?

Master Your Mind

Make your heart light

so your mind can be clear.

We are all making decisions

from our level of strength or weakness.

What decision will you make today?

Every life is born with the answer for it.

The problem of the mind is that it doesn't recognize you as its

Master

"Everyday I contemplate my last day and simply make

the best of today, for tomorrow is not promised."

Even though I live on into eternity,

absolute happiness is what I live for today.

That cannot be destroyed.

Finding You

The absolute truth about you is you.
Spend more time discovering it.

Instead

Don't beat yourself up.

Just step up.

To conquer the enemy outside,

first conquer the enemy within:

Ignorance of true self.

Find peace in recognizing that every life is a great force.

That Was Easy

Most solutions are simple

but hard to apply.

For they require a willingness to change.

No Regrets

Let's create a great life

between birth and death.

So at the end there is no regret.

Love yourself more above the rest.

You cannot regret what you didn't experience.

Every problem is a gift for you to experience a bigger you.

Personal Responsibility

It's time for a bloodless revolution,

a human revolution.

Strive to be the best that you can be.

Solving problems is a measurement of your greatness.

Faith is beyond your mind

and the mind cannot provide faith.

The Pleasure of Pain

Pain can assist you to becoming who you are.

If you want the results,

be willing to do what's hard.

The problems you have are yours to solve.

Why?

Because they are your problems.

State of Origin

Happiness is your original state.

Unhappiness is something you create.

Make peace with your past.

Master Your Mind

The mind is a powerful tool but a terrible Master.

Be the Master of the tool,

your mind,

in order to live a fulfilling life.

For it contains existence and nonexistence.

Simply life and death.

Rationalizing and knowing what's not good for you,

does not make it better.

In your mind is your body,

In your body is your mind,

and your spirit is in them all.

No Worries, No Regrets

In worrying about tomorrow and regretting yesterday,
there is no power or wisdom to deal with the present, today.
Put fear, worry, resentment, arrogance, and regret
out of your focus.
It is only the mind trying to steal your life-force.

Change

Sound and vibration break through barriers.

Chanting changes your circumstances.

Time is not the issue.

Faith is the promise.

When faith is consistent,

the drop of water will break down the boulder.

Simply persevere.

Pledge to Self

Let's make a pledge:
I am the observer of the thoughts in the mind
and I only entertain those
that encourage me to manifest my best.
Therefore, being the master of my mind
all the time
contributes to the world being a better place
for the entire human race.

Never Say "I'll Try"

Trying is faint-hearted.
Determination is whole-hearted.

No Excuses

Strong people don't make excuses.

They simply accept what is and make changes as necessary.

Know Thy Self

To know the truth of your self

and not exercise that truth

is a crime against your own humanity.

Because from beginning to end

you are the truth.

Truth in Beauty

Seek the beauty

in every experience.

Then there is nothing to complain about,

only more to discover.

Entitlement

Entitlement is dependence with an attitude.

You Are More

Believe in yourself

more than your difficult circumstances.

The truth about you

is beyond what you are thinking.

Be Still

The discovery of self

evokes the greatest joy.

Life goes beyond your presence and understanding.

Be still

and allow life to reveal your hidden truth.

Sit and contemplate.

Then you will know what to do.

For in doing

we illuminate a great experience.

To Complain

When you complain,

you are disparaging your life.

Appreciate life simply for the sunshine every day.

Start there.

You will feel better.

Self-Worth

Peace of mind is gold. Chaos is scrap metal.

Time moves forward and not backwards or still to complete the circle of life.

Maximum

Trying isn't maximum effort.

Determination is a full commitment.

Clarity

The power of evil is distraction. The power of good is clarity.

Choose wisely.

The Burden

Stop playing the tape of what happened in the past

and determine what you want to happen now.

It will only keep you in a state of dis-ease and negativity.

Change the present now for a better future.

Be present now.

About the Author

With more than 25 years of experience working in the healing arts, Adil Panton helps his clients break through innumerable physical, emotional and energetic obstacles by providing healing touch, wisdom, insight and life-changing guidance.

Born in Cuba, Adil was sent by his parents at two years old to live with his grandparents and six cousins in Kingston, Jamaica. It was the height of the Cuban Revolution. His parents fled to New York City where they worked to provide for their only child. Adil reunited with them in Brooklyn, New York 9 years later. As a massage therapist, Health Coach, Qigong and Tai Chi instructor.

After his first professional massage, he experienced an awakening. He realized first-hand that trauma stored in the body could be released through healing touch. The treatment naturally restored balance in his body's physical and energetic systems unknowingly traumatized years earlier when he was separated from his parents. At that moment, he understood his calling.

As a massage therapist, Health Coach and Qigong instructor, Adil uses his gifts of intuition and body work to realign, ease suffering and inspire change, assisting his clients' healing process in a wholistic and profound way.

At a young age, Adil took to heart his mother's advice. "If I could give you only one gift, it would be to trust your common sense," she said. After studying massage and Eastern philosophies, his gifts of providing guidance and insight are based on the common sense he learned to trust as a child.

Adil has penned the gift of common sense into each line in this gem-filled book of poetry. The reader will find themselves revealed, supported, encouraged and changed forever.

As a practicing SGI-Buddhist in Southern California, Adil operates a successful massage and wellness practice called Healing Arts Touch in Lake Forest. He specializes in individualized care and intuitive attention to each client's healthcare needs.

"All life is precious and deserves happiness."
- Adil Panton

CPSIA information can be obtained
at www.ICGtesting.com
Printed in the USA
LVHW100724221221
706813LV00002B/25